Best Easy Day Hikes Series

Best Easy Day Hikes San Gabriel Valley

Allen Riedel

FALCONGUIDES

GUILFORD, CONNECTICUT
HELENA, MONTANA

AN IMPRINT OF THE GLOBE PEQUOT PRESS

For Sierra, Makaila, and Michael

FALCONGUIDES®

Maps: OffRoute Inc. © Morris Book Publishing, LLC
TOPO! Explorer software and SuperQuad source maps courtesy of
National Geographic Maps. For information about TOPO! Explorer,
TOPO!, and Nat Geo Maps products, go to www.topo.com or www.nat
geomaps.com.

Library of Congress Cataloging-in-Publication Data
Riedel, Allen.
  Best easy day hikes, San Gabriel Valley / Allen Riedel.
    p. cm. – (Best easy day hikes series)
  ISBN 978-0-7627-5258-4
  1. Hiking–California–San Gabriel River Valley–Guidebooks. 2. San
Gabriel River Valley (Calif.)–Guidebooks. I. Title.
  GV199.42.C22S275 2009
  917.94'930454–dc22

                                              200902253
Printed in the United States of America

10 9 8 7 6 5 4 3 2 1

Contents

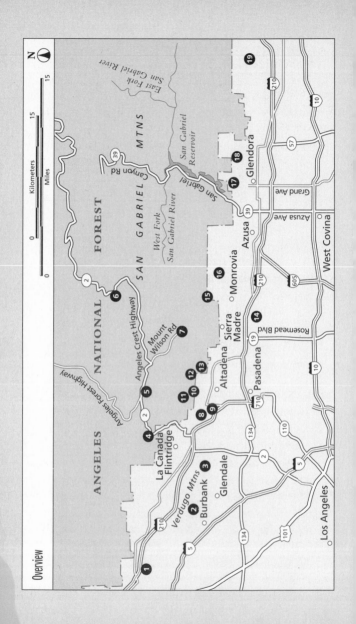

Overview

N

ANGELES NATIONAL FOREST

SAN GABRIEL NATIONAL FOREST

SAN GABRIEL MTNS

East Fork San Gabriel River

West Fork San Gabriel River

San Gabriel Reservoir

San Gabriel River

Canyon Rd

Angeles Crest Highway

Angeles Forest Highway

Mount Wilson Rd

Kilometers

Miles

0   15

0   15

La Cañada Flintridge

Verdugo Mtns

Burbank

Glendale

Altadena

Sierra Madre

Pasadena

Monrovia

Azusa

Glendora

West Covina

Los Angeles

Rosemead Blvd

Grand Ave

Azusa Ave

210

2

5

134

101

110

2

710

134

19

605

10

210

19

39

39

17

18

19

57

10

Acknowledgments

I would like to first and foremost thank all of the people who have spent time hiking with me in the mountains, deserts, hills, forests, jungles, and coastal beaches. Many of you, my friends, have inspired me in countless ways, and I can't thank you enough. I would like to mention some of you by name: Monique Riedel, Sean Coolican, Adam Mendelsohn, Cameron Alston, Bill Buck, Matt Piazza, Bruno Lucidarme, Chrissy Ziburski, Eric Walther, Bob Romano, Michael Millenheft III, Sierra Riedel, Makaila Riedel, Jim Zuber, Danny Suarez, Dylan Riedel, Eric Romero, Donn DeBaun, Alex Wilson, Dawn Wilson, and Jane Weal.

I would also like to acknowledge my family: Monique, Michael, Sierra, and Makaila—all four of you have spent lots of time with me on trails that were great and some "not so much" . . . I love you with all my heart.

I also owe a lot to my mom and dad, Barbara and Elmer Riedel, who raised me to believe in myself. Thanks! Thanks to my brother, Larry, and my grandparents, Herbert and Vivian Ward, Lucille Riedel, Elmer A. Riedel and my in-laws, Anna and Richard Chavez. I am a better person because of all of you.

I am also grateful for the opportunities that I have been granted by writing for the most amazing Web site: www .localhikes.com. Jim Zuber has been my biggest resource in the writing world, and I can never thank him enough for the awesome site and the amount of work he has sent my way. You rule, Jim!

I would like to thank Dave Ammenheuser and Patricia Mays at the *Press-Enterprise*. They are great editors and incredible people to work for.

I would like to thank Scott Adams and the wonderful people at The Globe Pequot Press, as well as my other publisher, The Mountaineers Books. Ashley, Kate, Carol, and everyone there have always been spectacular.

I would also like to thank Scott Ammons and all the wonderful people at REI for getting me started as an Outdoor School instructor.

Lastly I would like to thank all of the students and teachers I have worked with over the past ten years. It has been great knowing all of you.

Map Legend

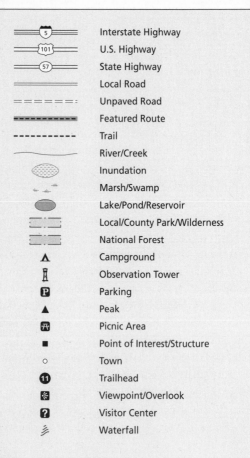

	Interstate Highway
	U.S. Highway
	State Highway
	Local Road
	Unpaved Road
	Featured Route
	Trail
	River/Creek
	Inundation
	Marsh/Swamp
	Lake/Pond/Reservoir
	Local/County Park/Wilderness
	National Forest
▲	Campground
	Observation Tower
℗	Parking
▲	Peak
	Picnic Area
■	Point of Interest/Structure
○	Town
⑪	Trailhead
	Viewpoint/Overlook
❓	Visitor Center
	Waterfall

Introduction

This book contains nineteen easy day hikes situated in and around the San Gabriel Valley. The hikes are located in a variety of locations, ranging from county, city, and/or local parks to the Angeles National Forest. The best short and easy hikes in the region, covering a vast range of scenery, historical interest, and natural beauty, are highlighted.

Some of the greatest hiking in Southern California exists within a thirty- to ninety-minute drive from the city center of Pasadena. The book is intended to be a sampling of the region, providing families, beginning hikers, and those with only a short amount of time or energy an introduction to the incredible wonders that the area has to offer.

Unbeknownst to many outside of the region, the San Gabriel Valley contains a great deal of austere and captivating pastoral beauty, from the chaparral-covered slopes of the foothills of the Verdugo Mountains to the lush higher forests of the San Gabriel Mountains. Numerous nature preserves, reserves, and specially designated parks protect valuable ecosystems and wildlife ranging from the Los Angeles County Arboretum and Hahamongna Watershed Park to the recreational havens of wilderness parks such as Glendora and Claremont Hills.

The valley is named for the San Gabriel River, which flows from the highest reaches of the San Gabriel Mountains. Descending through the county of Los Angeles, the river empties into the Pacific Ocean just south and east of Long Beach. Centered around the suburban metropolis of Pasadena, the city serves as a geographic and cultural core for the San Gabriel Valley. The regal mountains dominating the northern skyline are a defining feature of not only the city of Pasadena, but of Los Angeles and the entire Southern California region itself.

The San Gabriel Valley is a conglomeration of cities, towns, and other incorporated areas. Primarily suburban, some of the cities in the region have a slower-paced feel than the usual Los Angeles County fare, but the region itself is much more heavily populated than other parts of the United States, and outsiders will not be able to tell much difference between the cities within the urban region and those in the suburbs.

Typically Southern Californian, the San Gabriel region is a semi-arid Mediterranean ecosystem ringed by mountains created by the tectonic forces of the San Andreas Fault. Seasonal arroyos dot the terrain and flow intermittently through steep rugged canyons. Varied species of mammals, reptiles, and amphibians inhabit the landscape. The flora of the region, mostly desert and coastal chaparral, can be magnificent in color, especially during certain times of the year and after a significant amount of rainfall. Oak and pine forests grow into the upper elevations.

Mammals abound in the mountainous regions, with larger creatures such as black bear and mule deer inhabiting the higher reaches. Mountain lions and coyotes prowl throughout most of the foothills, park, and mountain areas, occasionally making their way into populated regions. Not really presenting much of a danger, the habitat of these predators is not as threatened as in other areas of Southern California. Much of the region that could have been developed by real estate interests has been built upon for over a century, and the animals have been adapting to these conditions for quite some time. Smaller creatures and rodents such as squirrels, skunks, possums, and mice are also abundant.

Several dams and waterways exist in the San Gabriel Valley, and while there are no major stopping points along the Pacific Flyway, there are opportunities for bird-watching. The region's mostly man-made lakes offer sanctuary, recreation, and fishing, and over 400 species of birds can be spotted throughout the year.

Hiking is a popular activity in the region, especially in the early morning and evening during summertime, and throughout the day during fall, winter, and spring. Depending on the location, summer days can be pleasant at higher elevations and absolutely desiccating in lower climes.

Typically, the only animal in the region that is dangerous to humans is the rattlesnake, which during hotter months can be prevalent on certain trails. Do not walk through tall grasses or place hands or feet into hidden locations. Snakes are afraid of humans, and they understand the world through sensing vibrations. Snakes will typically be alerted and flee long before a human approaches on the trail. Rattlesnakes will only strike if threatened, so the best thing to do is back away or walk in a wide berth around them on the trail. Mountain lions and bears can present an uncommon but real danger: Making noise as you walk along the trail and hiking in groups can significantly reduce the chance of encounters with these creatures, even though such encounters are already very rare.

Insects are not normally a problem in the San Gabriel Valley, though after rains ticks can present themselves, as can mosquitoes and other pests. Flies and gnats can be slightly troublesome in wetter areas, but are not normally a common problem. A mild insect repellent should do the trick for most hikes, and dogs should be protected with proper vaccinations and pet medicines.

Weather

The San Gabriel Valley is mostly semi-arid, and the lower elevations can be stifling during the months of June, July, August, and September. Heat can be a factor any time of the year, though late October through May is generally mild even in the hottest parts of the region.

Rain is not the normal state of affairs in Southern California, and the San Gabriel Valley is no exception, receiving only between 10 and 12 inches of rain annually. The rainy season is typically from November to February, though showers are more likely during December and January. Most rainstorms are over as quickly as they begin, though the region does see periods of continuing rainfall during the winter.

The mountains present an entirely different climate and create weather patterns that are separate from the rest of the region. Summer thunderstorms can be a common occurrence in the highest elevations, though rainfall does not typically occur elsewhere in the region during the summer.

Summer temperatures can reach the triple digits, though the higher mountain ranges rarely make it above the 80s F. The best times of year to hike in the San Gabriel Valley outside of the mountains are fall through spring, when the temperatures are mild during the day. Early morning just before and after sunrise and evening just before and after sunset are pleasant in the summer almost anywhere.

Preparing for Your Hike

Before you go hiking, always be prepared. Let someone know where you are planning to go and leave an itinerary of your hiking destination with a reliable friend or family member. Give them an expected return time and the name of the trailhead you are visiting, along with specific routes you are taking. Be sure that your friend or family member will contact authorities should you not return as expected.

Water is essential in desert environments. Hydrate before you leave as well as during your hike, and leave extra water in your vehicle so that you can hydrate upon return. A good rule of thumb for hiking is one-half to one liter of water per hour of hiking, and on hot days without shade, one should drink as much as one gallon per hour of hiking. Salty snacks can help aid water retention. Hikers should avoid overexertion during the hottest part of the day.

When you hike, you should always bring along the so-called Ten Essentials so that you can provide yourself with the basic necessities for survival should the unexpected occur. Hiking is a relatively safe activity, especially when care is taken, although it is always best to prepare for any eventuality. Minor mishaps like taking a wrong turn, getting back after dark, or being lost for a short while can be frightening, but as long as cool heads prevail, most outdoor situations can be easily rectified. The Ten Essentials are a list designed to keep people safe and provide a backup plan should something go wrong:

1. Navigation (map, compass, GPS)
2. Sun protection (hat, sunscreen)
3. Insulation (layered clothing)

4. Illumination (head lamp, flashlight)
5. First-aid supplies (Band-Aids, bandages, gauze, tape, tweezers, etc.)
6. Repair kit and tools (knife, duct tape, etc.)
7. Nutrition (extra food)
8. Hydration (extra water)
9. Emergency shelter (tarp, tent, sleeping bag, or emergency blanket)
10. Fire starter (necessary for life-threatening emergencies only)

Please note: The San Gabriel Valley is an extremely arid region and wildfire is a constant danger and threat. Fires are not permitted in parks, forests, and hiking areas outside of designated campgrounds and Yellow Post campsites. If a life-threatening emergency is present, an area must be cleared 8 feet in diameter around the fire and a rock ring should be constructed to contain the fire itself. Lighting a fire, however, is not recommended nor endorsed by this book.

This is only a basic list and, of course, other items may also be of use. The list can be modified according to the amount of time a hiker spends on the trail. Some items may be deemed more important than others.

Clothing and Gear

Clothing should be made up of layers to protect one's body from the elements, whether wind, heat, rain, or cold. An insulating layer of water and sweat-wicking fabric (polyester, neoprene, Capilene, or other synthetic fiber) is best for a basic layer. These fabrics wick sweat away from your body and keep you warm. On hot days cotton can be a good choice because the sweat will remain on the fabric, keeping you cooler than a synthetic material. But cotton is a bad choice for cold and rainy days because the material retains water and loses its ability to insulate, which in even less than extreme circumstances can lead to hypothermia.

A fleece shell is good for an insulating layer because the material is lightweight and dries quickly. On days without a hint of precipitation, a fleece jacket may be the only necessary outerwear to bring along.

Lastly, a lightweight rain shell should be brought along in case of emergencies. Rain and snow can be deadly in the mountains. A waterproof shell and pants offer protection from the elements.

Improvements in lightweight hiking boots and shoes over the past decade have revolutionized the sport. Boots no longer need to be bulky, heavy, cumbersome Frankenstein-like appendages that cause blisters, chafing, and sore feet. Instead, many outdoor specialty shops can measure a hiker's feet and find a great-fitting shoe that can be worn immediately on the trail. These shoes are durable, sturdy, and excellent for short day hikes, although they may not be ideal for longer and more difficult trekking.

Socks made of wool or synthetic materials are best because they take moisture away from the feet, reducing chafing and blisters.

Backpacks for day hiking should be small, fit comfortably, and carry between 10 and 20 pounds. Carrying more than 20 pounds on a day hike is actually kind of silly, and will probably only serve to make the experience less enjoyable. In today's ultra-light market, weeklong backpacking trips can be made carrying only 20 to 25 pounds (water and food included) so find a backpack that is large enough to carry what is needed, but light enough to be comfortable. Hydration systems have become the norm, and drinking from a reservoir tube is pure bliss compared to the days of cumbersome canteens or stopping to retrieve water bottles from a pack when thirsty.

Trail Regulations/Restrictions

Trails in this guide are located in national forests, preserves, and local or regional parks. Trails located in the national forest require an Adventure Pass for parking. Daily or annual passes may be purchased at sporting goods stores, specialty outdoor shops, and in the local mountains. Access to some city parks and natural areas is free while others require day-use fees. Fees for trailhead usage are not required anywhere, though camping permits may carry fees.

Zero Impact

Trails in the San Gabriel area and neighboring foothills are heavily used year-round. We, as trail users and advocates, must be especially vigilant to make sure our passage leaves no lasting mark. Here are some basic guidelines for preserving trails in the region:

Pack out all your own trash, including biodegradable items like orange peels and sunflower seeds. In the arid Southern California climate, items such as these take ten or more years to decompose. If everyone who hiked these trails left peels and shells behind, the trails would look more like a waste dump than a forest or wild landscape. You might also pack out garbage left by less considerate hikers—take a plastic bag and make the place better for your having been there.

Don't approach or feed any wild creatures—the ground squirrel eyeing your snack food is best able to survive if it remains self-reliant.

Don't pick wildflowers or gather rocks, antlers, feathers, or other treasures along the trail. Removing these items will only take away from the next hiker's experience.

Remain on the established route to avoid damaging trailside soils and plants. This is also a good rule of thumb for avoiding poison oak and stinging nettle, common regional trailside irritants.

Don't cut switchbacks, which can promote erosion. Be courteous by not making loud noises while hiking.

Many of these trails are multiuse, which means you'll share them with other hikers, trail runners, mountain bikers, and equestrians. Familiarize yourself with proper trail etiquette, yielding the trail when appropriate. When in doubt, be courteous and simply let other users pass.

Use outhouses at trailheads or along the trail.

The Falcon Zero-Impact Principles

- Leave with everything you brought with you.
- Leave no sign of your visit.
- Leave the landscape as you found it.

Play It Safe

Generally, hiking in and around the San Gabriel Valley is a safe and fun way to explore the outdoors. Hiking is not without its risks, but there are ways to reduce those risks, and following a few simple steps and guidelines will help to make the activity as benign as possible.

It is a good idea to know simple first aid, including how

to treat bleeding, bites and stings, and fractures, strains, or sprains. Make sure to take along at least a basic first-aid kit. It won't help to have the skills if you don't have any supplies.

The San Gabriel Valley, and Southern California for that matter, is known for its sunny skies and warm climate. The sun can be powerful, especially at higher elevations: Use sunscreen and wear a wide-brimmed hat. Weather patterns can change abruptly, especially in the mountains and during winter and spring months (November through April). Carry properly layered clothing items to protect yourself from temperature changes and rain. Remember, summer thunderstorms aren't uncommon in the mountains and may bring dangers such as freezing temperatures, lightning, hail, and high winds.

The hills and mountains are home to a variety of wildlife. Some can be host to disease, and others may attack if prompted by hunger or the smell of food. Rattlesnakes may be found on any of the hikes described, particularly from early spring to mid-fall. Be careful where you place your hands and feet.

Learn how to spot and identify poison oak. Its appearance will change throughout the year. During spring and summer the distinctive three-pronged leaf may appear green and then turn to red and brown as the season progresses into winter. In winter the leaves may completely fall off the plant, leaving a hard-to-identify stalk that still contains and spreads the toxins when touched by human skin. The noxious plant grows abundantly near water, in the canyons, and along the hillsides.

Ticks are another pest to be avoided. They are more likely to be found near water or after rains. They hang in the brush waiting to drop on warm-blooded animals. It is a good idea to check for ticks every time you pause along the trail. Ticks will generally hang on to clothing or hair and not bite until the host has stopped moving. Remove them before they have a chance to bite.

The San Gabriel Valley is almost a desert ecosystem and temperatures can soar, so bring more drinking water than you think you'll need. Any water you find on these hikes is generally considered unsafe to drink if untreated. Boil, filter, or treat this water before consumption.

Other items may be fun to have along as well. Cameras can be used to record an excursion for posterity. Binoculars can come in handy for wildlife viewing. Plant, bird, animal, and insect identification guides can prove to be informative and educational. Handheld global positioning satellite units are becoming more and more inexpensive and are a great tool to use on the trail. Maps should be taken, but most trails are well marked.

Trail Finder

Best Hikes for Children

Best Hikes for Waterfalls

Best Hikes for Views

Best Hikes for Nature

Hansen Dam Recreation Area

The Hansen Dam Recreation Area is operated by Los Angeles County Parks and Recreation. The park offers many opportunities for outdoor activities, including boating, hiking, swimming, and horseback riding. A golf course, baseball diamonds, picnic areas, and other facilities are also available at the location.

1 Hansen Dam

Take a stroll through wetlands in the Tujunga watershed and enjoy an historic dam with fantastic opportunities for bird-watching.

Distance: 4-mile loop
Approximate hiking time: 2 hours
Elevation gain: 40 feet
Trail surface: Packed dirt, dirt road
Best season: Fall through spring; winter can be wet, summer can be hot
Other trail users: Joggers, dogs, horses, bicycles
Canine compatibility: Leashed dogs permitted

Fees and permits: None
Maps: *USGS San Fernando, CA Topo,* CD 9
Contact: Los Angeles County Parks and Recreation—Hansen Dam Recreation Area, 11770 Foothill Blvd., Lake View Terrace, CA 91342; (818) 899-6016 or (818) 896-6215; www.laparks .org/dos/reccenter/facility/ hansendamRC.htm

Finding the trailhead: From the junction of Interstate 210 and Highway 134, take I-210 west for 17.3 miles to exit 8 for Osborne Street. Turn left onto Foothill Boulevard and drive for 0.2 mile. Turn left into the parking area for the dam. GPS: N 34 16.23' / W 118 22.56'

The Hike

Hansen Dam was completed in 1940 after horrendous floods wreaked havoc on Los Angeles in 1934 and 1938. Major infrastructure and thousands of homes were destroyed during the deluges. Many people lost their lives, and the floods eventually led the United States Congress to enact the Flood Control Act of 1941. The Hansen Dam was and is the cornerstone that stops catastrophic flooding in the Southland.

Today there is little left to remind visitors of the dam's great importance. Hemmed in by small ranches, housing developments, freeways, and urban areas, the dam and its park and recreation area are a slice of peace and serenity.

Home to baseball diamonds, picnic areas, public swimming, and a host of various other outdoor activities, the Hansen Dam Recreation Area is a getaway for urbanites looking for recreation. However, less well known are the miles of trails that loop through the park and the Big Tujunga Wash to the east. There are multiple trails, some of which are large and maintained, while others are created by hikers traveling off-trail and crisscross the main path. Equestrians and dog lovers frequent the region, and there are sections of path that are lovely and wooded. Spotting wildlife is a common occurrence and bird-watchers will feel at home.

This route follows the inside loop around the dam on mostly dirt path and roads, but does cross some pavement along the way. With the confluence of multiple paths, it is difficult to stay on the correct route for this entire trip, but walking along the widest path in a loop from east to west around the major basins will help keep those looking to follow the main route on track. Further exploration is also a possibility. The area is large, but not so large that you'll get lost. This route traverses the margins of the Tujunga Wash, where the riparian habitat can be quite lovely.

From the parking area, head south and walk along the wide dirt path for 0.25 mile. Pass four baseball diamonds and turn right onto the wide dirt path that follows along Hansen Lake. At the fork, turn left and stay close the shoreline, where the path will significantly widen. At 0.5 mile turn right onto a much smaller path and follow it west and south

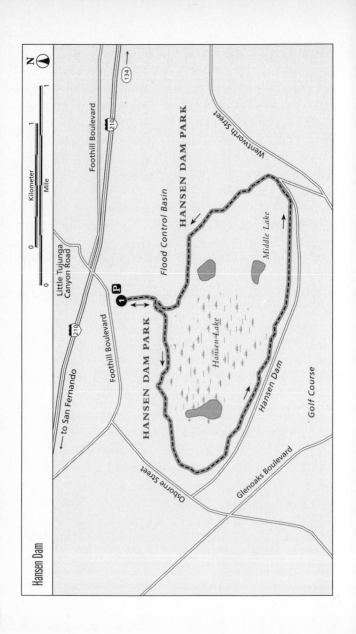

around the edge of a smaller portion of the lake. At just over a mile, the base of the dam can be seen. Follow the trail to the base and stay just beside the dam for nearly 2 miles of hiking. At 2.75 miles the trail forks again—follow the left path. Streams do flow into the lake, but they are mostly very placid. Cross over the main stream on rocks placed by other hikers at 3.25 miles. At 3.5 miles turn left onto the main dirt path. This leads back to the baseball diamonds. Turn right and return to the parking area.

Miles and Directions

0.0 Head south from the parking area past four baseball diamonds.

0.25 Turn right and head west along the main trail.

0.35 Turn left at the fork and follow the shoreline.

0.5 Turn right onto a smaller trail.

1.0 Walk south toward the dam and the main trail. Follow the dam wall for nearly 2 miles.

2.75 Turn left at the fork.

3.25 Cross the stream.

3.5 Turn right onto the path that leads back to the parking area.

4.0 Return to the parking area.

Verdugo Mountains

The Verdugo Mountains, or Verdugo Hills, are a subsidiary range of the San Gabriel Mountains. They stretch from Pasadena's western border to the San Fernando Valley. The separating valley between the higher San Gabriels to the north is properly known as the Crescenta Valley, which opens up into the greater San Gabriel Valley to the east.

The mountains were named for a prominent land-owning family that controlled the region and a good piece of greater Los Angeles County during the late 1700s. Several protected parcels of land dot the small range, and different agencies control various regions of the mountains, ranging from the privately owned to local and state parks. Most of the range is covered in fire roads, though smaller trails exist within the parks themselves.

2 Wildwood Canyon Park

Hike in the spacious Verdugo Mountains at Wildwood Canyon Park. The canyon is peaceful, shady, and idyllic, while mountain trails lead to spectacular viewpoints.

Distance: 2-mile loop
Approximate hiking time: 1 hour
Elevation gain: 700 feet
Trail surface: Packed dirt and pavement
Best season: Year-round, although summers can be hot
Other trail users: Joggers, strollers, wheelchairs, bicycles, dogs
Canine compatibility: Leashed dogs permitted

Regulations: Open sunrise to 30 minutes after sunset
Fees and permits: None
Maps: *USGS Burbank, CA Topo,* CD 9
Contact: Santa Monica Mountains Conservancy, 1701 Wildwood Canyon Drive, Burbank, CA 91501; (818) 238-5440; www.lamountains.com/parks .asp?parkid=647

Finding the trailhead: From the junction of Interstate 210 and Highway 134, take Highway 134 west for 7.9 miles to Interstate 5, and exit north toward Sacramento. Drive for 3.5 miles to exit 146B onto West Burbank Boulevard. Drive for 0.5 mile, then turn right onto North Third Street. Turn left at East Harvard Road and drive for 1.6 miles. Park in the large lot to the west of the entrance. GPS: N 34 12.12' / W 118 17.52'

The Hike

Wildwood Canyon Park is a wonderful gem nestled between two ridgelines in the Verdugo Mountains. Replete with sculptures and monogrammed stonework, the park is beautifully landscaped. The entrance is modern, warm, and

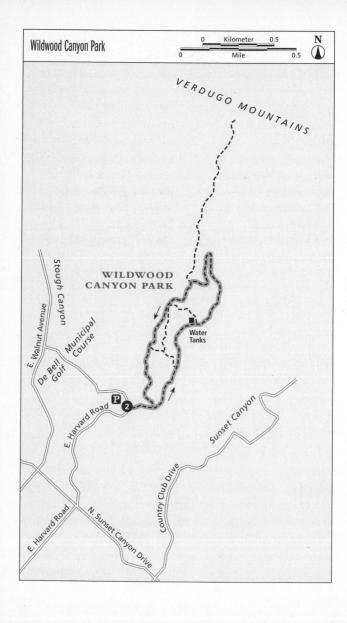

Wildwood Canyon Park

0 Kilometer 0.5

0 Mile 0.5

N

VERDUGO MOUNTAINS

WILDWOOD
CANYON PARK

Stough Canyon

E. Walnut Avenue

De Bell Golf
Municipal Course

Water Tanks

P 2

E. Harvard Road

Sunset Canyon

Country Club Drive

E. Harvard Road

N. Sunset Canyon Drive

inviting. The interior of the park is truly beautiful, wild yet accessible, and serves as a fabulous example of an urban park planned and implemented properly. This hike explores both the western ridge of the parkland and the lovely tranquil canyon that is designated by its inspired namesake.

From the parking area, head up the roadway for 0.1 mile, where the trailhead begins next to an explicit and thoroughly detailed placard/map of the park and its trails. The city of Burbank left nothing to chance or misinterpretation with this map and its legend. Turn left and follow the trail as it snakes its way up the crest of the mountain. The trail is wide and easy to follow for its entire route, and a connector trail can be followed to the uppermost reaches of the range; those wishing to continue hiking may do so, though the scope and difficulty of such a hike is not covered here. Instead the route described here follows the park map. There isn't much shade along the crest, so hot days are best avoided.

Several trails intersect the main trail, but the route is easy to follow, and those who are interested in hiking a smaller loop can take one of the two cutoff trails and return via the roadway. However, this trip is best enjoyed as a 2-mile round-trip loop. The trail gains elevation rather steeply for the first half mile, climbing 600 feet in that short distance. This will be enough to take the breath away from most hikers, and use of rest stops is encouraged, but the views are well worth the effort and the workout is superb. The top of the trail is reached in a little less than a mile, and from this vantage point a beautiful panorama opens up of the Los Angeles Basin and the city of Burbank. The Verdugo Mountains tower to the north, while the southern views are open to the wonderful blue of the Pacific Ocean. The best views occur in winter when the skies are clear. This is also a great place to watch the sun set over the sea.

From the high point on the trail, follow the right fork and begin the descent into the canyon. The return route meanders through the lovely canyon. Follow the road back to the parking lot. If the day is warm, hikers may wish to reverse the route so that the uphill trek is undertaken in the shade.

Miles and Directions

0.0 Head north along the roadway.

0.1 Turn left and follow the trail up the ridge.

0.4 Reach the first cutoff trail, continue left.

0.6 Reach second cutoff trail, continue left.

0.7 Reach third cutoff trail, continue left.

0.8 Reach connector trail to uppermost ridgeline, continue right to high point of trail.

0.9 Arrive at high point and enjoy the view.

1.25 Trail becomes Wildwood Canyon Road.

2.0 Return to the parking area.

3 South Verdugo Mountain

Hike along a fire road to the highest reaches of the Verdugo Mountains and experience amazing views of the entire Southland.

Distance: 5.5-mile loop
Approximate hiking time: 3 hours
Elevation gain: 1,400 feet
Trail surface: Packed dirt
Best season: Fall through spring; hot in summer
Other trail users: Dogs, bicycles, joggers, horses

Canine compatibility: Leashed dogs permitted
Fees and permits: None
Maps: *USGS Del Mar, CA Topo, CD 9*
Contact: Glendale Parks and Recreation, 613 E. Broadway, Room 120, Glendale, CA 91206; (818) 548-2000; http://parks .ci.glendale.ca.us/

Finding the trailhead: From the junction of Interstate 210 and Highway 134, take I-210 west for 7.8 miles to exit 17, La Crescenta Avenue. Turn left and drive for 1.0 mile. Turn right onto Oakmont View Drive and drive for 0.6 mile. Turn left onto Barnes Circle and drive for 0.3 mile. Turn right onto Beaudry Terrace and drive for 0.1 mile. Park on the street. GPS: N 34 11.37' / W 118 14.27'

The Hike

Perched atop the highest reaches of the city of Glendale sits the easternmost boundary of the Verdugo Mountains. The foothill range is isolated and austere, but locked in and totally encircled by the city. Stretching for 6.0 miles, the hills are loaded with wildlife, spectacular views, and great opportunities for outdoor recreation. This hike is absolutely

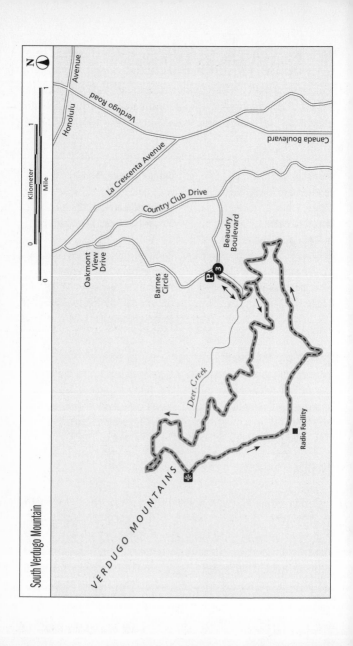

South Verdugo Mountain

no exception to that rule, and if the skies are clear, expect to be dazzled.

The hike takes place on two fire roads that loop together into one giant adventure. The northern road is substantially shadier than the southern one, so taking a counterclockwise route avoids most of the sun, which can be problematic and worsened by the climb required during the first half of either route. That's not to say the northern road is "shady": It is a wide fire road dotted with intermittent clusters of oaks and scrub, but it does provide more opportunities for shade than the southern road, especially in the morning, due to its north-side orientation.

From Beaudry Boulevard, walk up the dirt road beyond the gate and hike to a junction almost half a mile into the hike. Take the northern (right) branch onto the unsigned fire road. The views begin immediately into the San Gabriel Mountains and the Crescenta Valley. At 2.5 miles head south on the left fork and walk up the road toward the towers that loom overhead. The towers are the high point of the hike and a bench has been placed on the southern slope so that weary soles/souls may take a break and enjoy the Los Angeles cityscape and skyline. Truly, the vistas are magnificent; on the clearest of days, the Channel Islands can be seen glittering on the bright blue of the Pacific Ocean and a vibrant panorama of the entire Southland stretches toward the horizon.

Hike south for another half mile and take the far left path at the three-way fork, this route continues until the intersection near the end of the trail. The views abide for most of the remaining trip and the gentle downhill gradient is pleasant and enjoyable. At 5.2 miles continue straight and right back onto Beaudry North Motorway toward Beaudry Boulevard.

Miles and Directions

0.0 From the street, head west and up to the dirt road at the corner of Beaudry Boulevard and Beaudry Terrace.

0.1 Pass the gate blocking vehicular traffic.

0.45 Take the right fork onto Beaudry North Motorway.

2.5 Take the left fork onto Beaudry South Motorway. Head toward the radio towers.

3.0 Arrive at the radio towers and high point of the hike.

3.5 Turn onto the far left road at the three-way fork.

5.2 Turn right to return to Beaudry North Motorway and return to Beaudry Boulevard.

5.5 Arrive at Beaudry Boulevard.

Angeles National Forest–Angeles Crest Highway

The Angeles National Forest stretches from the Newhall Pass in the west to San Bernardino County in the east. The San Gabriel Mountains continue into the Cajon Pass and Interstate 15. The mountain range is further comprised of two sets of mountains, a taller northern range and the front range, which looms high above the San Gabriel Valley.

The mountains were named for the river of the same name that flows from out of the mountains 75 miles to the Pacific Ocean. The Angeles Crest Highway enters the mountains in La Canada just north and west of Pasadena and divides the mountains in half, exiting onto Highway 138 near Interstate 15 in the high desert. Ample opportunity for outdoor activities exists along the highway. The hikes in this book only sample the lower country close to Pasadena, but no matter the destination, wild adventure awaits.

4 Grizzly Flat / Vasquez Creek

Distance: 5.75-mile lollipop
Approximate hiking time: 3 hours
Elevation gain: 1,300 feet
Trail surface: Packed dirt
Best season: Fall through spring; summers are hot
Other trail users: Joggers, bicyclists, dogs, horses
Canine compatibility: Leashed dogs allowed

Fees and permits: Adventure Pass required
Maps: *USGS Condor Peak, CA Topo*, CD 9
Contact: Angeles National Forest, 701 N. Santa Anita Ave., Arcadia, CA 91006; (626) 574-5200; www.fs.fed.us/r5/angeles/

Finding the trailhead: From the junction of Interstate 210 and Highway 134, take I-210 west for 5.2 miles to the Angeles Crest Highway/Highway 2 exit. Turn left onto Angeles Crest Highway and drive for 6.1 miles and park in the large turnout and parking area on the west (left) side of the highway. The trailhead begins to the south of the parking area on Forest Road 2N79. GPS: 34 15.37' / W 118 11.29'

The Hike

The hike to Grizzly Flat is mainly on an easily graded fire road. Vehicle access is limited to the occasional forest service truck, but the road is gated and blocked off to any public use other than that operated by foot power. Mountain bikers, equestrians, and people with pets all use the trail, though it isn't immensely popular. The lower regions of the Angeles Forest are quite underused and this trail is no exception.

The beauty of this hike is understated. Oaks line the roadway and views are intermittent as the trail climbs gently into the forest. The region is rife with local history, and the moniker for the hike comes from the bear that adorns the

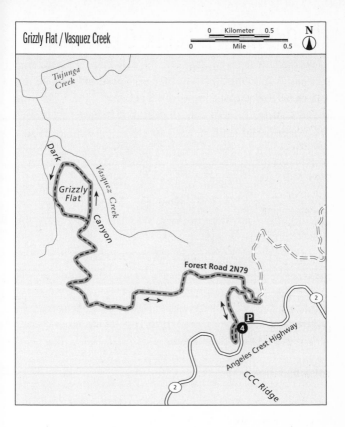

Tujunga Creek

Dark

Grizzly Flat

Vasquez Creek

Canyon

Forest Road 2N79

P

4

Angeles Crest Highway

CCC Ridge

2

2

state flag of California. Yes, merely 150 years ago the entire forest was abundant with the majestic beasts. The grizzly bear's eventual extinction in Southern California came less than one hundred years ago, and the only evidence of them now survives on trails and locales with names such as these.

Also of historical significance are tales of the notorious California bandit Tiburcio Vasquez. Various locations around the Southland are named for his exploits, and Vasquez Creek meanders just to the east of Grizzly Flat.

Vasquez and his men were said to have used the rugged canyons to escape from lawmen chasing them from one nefarious crime to another. At his trial Vasquez attributed the motivation for his crimes, which included robberies, murders, and general chaos, to a desire to free California from the grasp of the United States and return it to Mexico. This gained him fame and respect among like-minded individuals, but it is unclear whether his intentions and anarchy were truly moved by such a calling.

In a little less than a mile, the roadway reaches the crest and its highest point. Here the views stretch from the depths of Big Tujunga Canyon to the high mountains to the north and east. Grizzly Flat is easily recognizable from the top because it was once used as a pine plantation by the forest service to replace trees in other regions of the forest. The road drops 800 feet down into Dark Canyon and eventually becomes a trail at 2.5 miles. Hikers can explore the grove of tall planted pines, which seem very out of place in this part of the forest.

Return via the same route.

Miles and Directions

- **0.0** From the parking area, head south up gated Forest Road 2N79.
- **0.5** Reach a road junction; continue left.
- **0.8** Cross a ridgeline firebreak, continue right.
- **1.2** Cross ridgeline firebreak again, continue right.
- **1.5** Arrive at a road junction, take the first road on the right.
- **2.5** Arrive at Grizzly Flat, road becomes trail. Walk around the pine plantation.
- **3.25** Return to road and retrace route back to parking area.
- **5.75** Arrive at the parking area.

5 Switzer Falls

Hike through an enchanted canyon to a lovely waterfall.

Distance: 3.4 miles out and back

Approximate hiking time: 2 hours

Elevation gain: 500 feet

Trail surface: Packed dirt

Best season: After winter and spring rains, year-round

Other trail users: Dogs

Canine compatibility: Leashed dogs permitted

Fees and permits: Adventure Pass required

Maps: *USGS Condor Peak, CA Topo,* CD 9

Contact: Angeles National Forest, 701 N. Santa Anita Ave., Arcadia, CA 91006; (626) 574-5200; www.fs.fed.us/r5/angeles/

Finding the trailhead: From the junction of Interstate 210 and Highway 134, take I-210 west for 5.2 miles to the Angeles Crest Highway/Highway 2 exit. Turn left onto Angeles Crest Highway and drive for 9.7 miles. Turn right at Switzer Truck Trail and drive for 0.5 mile to the day-use Switzer Picnic Area parking. GPS: N 34 15.59' / W 118 08.42'

The Hike

From the parking area, walk down the roadway and cross the footbridge that spans Arroyo Seco. This is the beginning of the well-worn and wide trail that leads to Switzer Falls. One of the more popular destinations in the lower part of the Angeles National Forest, the picnic area and the trail are often full of people, especially on weekends and holidays. It is, after all, just a short drive up from the city; and the beauty of this creek, its canyon, its falls, and the wooded

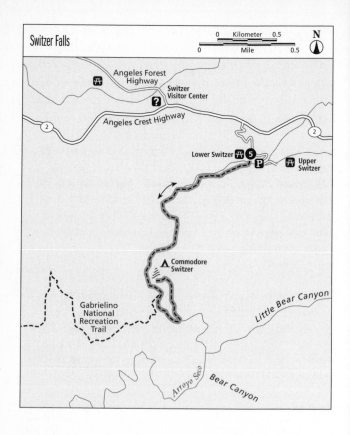

surroundings make it a favorite destination for many, who return here year after year.

The Arroyo Seco, which in Spanish literally means "dry creek," is a lovely riparian habitat filled with spruce, alder, willow, maple, and oak trees lining the walls of the canyon. The stream usually has some water in it year-round, but it dries up intermittently in places during warmer months. The best time to catch the falls is during wetter months and after winters with good snowfalls. Some creek crossing is required in spots, as the trail skirts the edge of the water. Follow the wide trail 1.0 mile to the remains of Switzer's Camp, an old resort from the "golden age" of hiking. Here an overlook of the falls provides a respite on the way down as well as back up.

The trek to the falls and beyond has been popular in the San Gabriel Mountains for as long as people have been hiking in the region. From the late 1800s through the mid-1900s, before the completion of the Angeles Crest Highway, visitors from the city hiked up the wild corridor from Pasadena to Switzer's Camp, which was a lavish resort frequented by movie stars and adventure seekers. Once the highway made access to the mountains commonplace, the once faraway resorts became a thing of the past. Almost nothing remains of the old buildings except some stone walls and foundations, but it is fun to explore.

From the camp, which is now a backcountry campsite, continue down and south toward Bear Canyon. In a little less than half a mile, turn left on the well-used but unmarked side trail that leads north back up the canyon 0.3 mile to the base of the falls.

Return via the same route. Do not attempt to hike down from the camp to the falls along the creek, as there are several sharp cascades and the mountainsides are unstable. There are many steep and dangerous drops. Hiking up the canyon walls from the falls is also inadvisable and dangerous. Stay on the trails.

Miles and Directions

0.0 From the picnic area, head southwest across the footbridge to the wide trail.

1.0 Reach old Switzer's Camp and an overlook of Switzer Falls.

1.2 Go left (east) onto the unmarked use trail that leads down into the canyon.

1.4 Turn left and head back upstream toward the base of the falls.

3.4 Arrive back at the picnic area.

6 Vetter Mountain Lookout

Climb to an historic fire lookout and learn about the flora of the region on the short Wolf Tree Nature Trail.

Distance: 2.75 miles out and back

Approximate hiking time: 2 hours

Elevation gain: 650 feet

Trail surface: Packed dirt

Best season: Year-round

Other trail users: Dogs

Canine compatibility: Leashed dogs permitted

Fees and permits: Adventure Pass required

Maps: *USGS Chilao Flat, CA Topo,* CD 9

Contact: Angeles National Forest, 701 N. Santa Anita Ave., Arcadia, CA 91006; (626) 574-5200; www.fs.fed.us/r5/angeles/

Finding the trailhead: From the junction of Interstate 210 and Highway 134, take I-210 west for 5.2 miles. Take the Angeles Crest Highway (Highway 2) exit. Turn right and drive for 23.0 miles. Turn left onto Forest Road 3N16 and make an immediate right onto 3N16.1, signed for lower Charlton Flats Picnic Area. Drive 0.5 mile to the day-use parking area and locked gate. If the gate is locked or parking is not available, park near the entrance and walk up the road to the trailhead. GPS: N 34 17.55' / W 118 00.50'

The Hike

From the parking area along Forest Road 3N16.1, walk south onto the trail marked for Vetter Mountain. This trail crosses through lovely wooded Charlton Flats and follows part of the 53–mile–long forest spanning Silver Moccasin Trail. It also encompasses the Wolf Tree Nature Trail in a semi–figure eight.

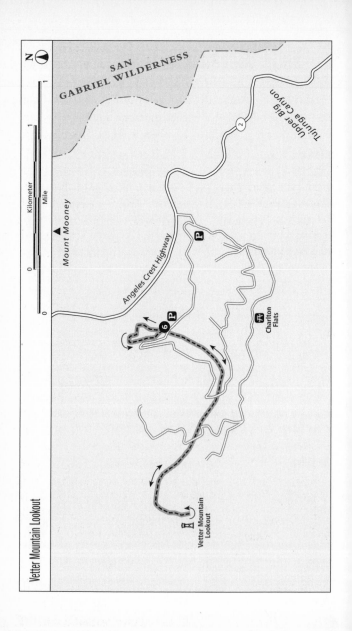

Vetter Mountain Lookout

SAN GABRIEL WILDERNESS

Mount Mooney

Angeles Crest Highway

Upper Big Tujunga Canyon

Charlton Flats

Vetter Mountain Lookout

N

0   1 Kilometer
0   1 Mile

The Charlton Flats region of the Angeles National Forest is at a convergence of the varying ecosystems that comprise the San Gabriel Mountains. At almost 6,000 feet, the forest's first pines start to crop up. Here they intermix with the desert chaparral that creeps up from the lower regions and create an amalgam of ecosystems that is interesting to explore.

Starting from lower Charlton Flats, head southwest on the Vetter Mountain Trail. At 0.2 mile stay straight at the junction with the Silver Moccasin Trail. Walking through lovely groves of pines, cedars, and firs, the area feels more remote than it actually is. The route begins to follow a very dry arroyo, which only moistens up during periods of rain. There are two road crossings in the next half mile. Simply cross the roadway both times and stay on the trail. The route meanders through mixed forest and climbs fairly gently to the summit.

At the top of Vetter Mountain is an historic forest lookout that was built in 1935. The lookout was in disuse for seven years and was renovated and reopened in 1998 by volunteers. These same volunteers now operate the lookout, along with many others throughout Southern California's forests, and friendly and informed staff can answer questions on weekends and most weekdays during peak fire months from May through November. From the catwalk around the lookout, enjoy amazing views of the San Gabriel Wilderness, the front range, and the higher back range of the San Gabriels. Big Tujunga Canyon drops to the west, and the views are fantastic for such minimal effort.

Return on the same trail to the parking area. At this point continue across the road on the Wolf Tree Nature Trail, which is a short jaunt. Here visitors can read the informational plaques and learn a bit about the forest. Return on the road to the parking area when finished.

Miles and Directions

0.0 Head southwest on the trail to Vetter Mountain/Silver Moccasin Trail.

0.2 Stay straight and to the right with the junction for the Silver Moccasin Trail.

0.4 Cross Forest Road 3N16.

0.6 Cross Forest Road 3N16A.

1.2 Reach Vetter Mountain Lookout. Return via the same route.

2.4 Arrive back at Forest Road 3N16.1. Head north across the road to the Wolf Tree Nature Trail. Follow the path counter-clockwise.

2.7 Intersect with Forest Road 3N16.1 (closed) and return south toward the parking area.

2.75 Return to the parking area.

7 Mount Wilson to Mount Harvard

Hike along the historic Mount Wilson Toll Road and climb to a peak with incredible views of the entire Southland.

Distance: 3.0 miles out and back

Approximate hiking time: 1.5 hours

Elevation gain: 800 feet

Trail surface: Packed dirt

Best season: Year-round, although summer days can be extremely hot and smoggy

Other trail users: Joggers, dogs, bicyclists

Canine compatibility: Leashed dogs permitted

Fees and permits: Adventure Pass required

Maps: USGS Mount Wilson, CA Topo, CD 9

Contact: Angeles National Forest, 701 N. Santa Anita Ave., Arcadia, CA 91006; (626) 574-5200; www.fs.fed.us/r5/angeles/

Finding the trailhead: From the junction of Interstate 210 and Highway 134, drive east on I-210 for 5.2 miles and exit onto Angeles Crest Highway/Highway 2. Turn right onto Highway 2 and drive for 13.8 miles to Red Box Junction. Turn right onto Forest Road 2N24/Mount Wilson/Red Box Road and drive for 4.3 miles. Turn right onto Mount Wilson Toll Road. Drive 0.3 mile down the one-way road to the limited parking next to the gate. GPS: N 34 13.30' / W 118 03.50'

The Hike

The San Gabriel Mountains are brimming with history. Mount Wilson is no exception. It's home to what used to be the largest telescope in the world. The facility is still in use as an observatory, and the solar observations that occur

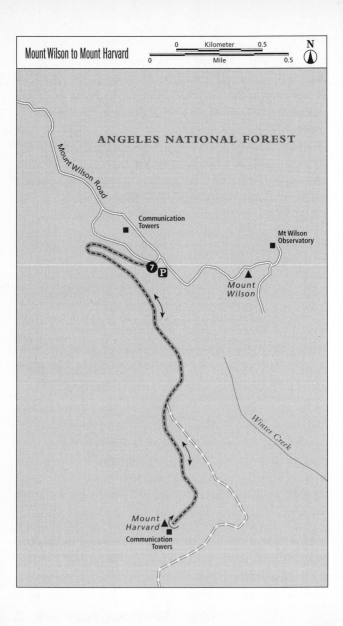

Mount Wilson to Mount Harvard

0   Kilometer   0.5

0   Mile   0.5

N

ANGELES NATIONAL FOREST

Mount Wilson Road

Communication Towers

Mt Wilson Observatory

7 P

Mount Wilson

Winter Creek

Mount Harvard
Communication Towers

there are the longest continuous monitorings of the sun anywhere on the planet. The radio towers that line the summit are almost as much of a landmark for the Southland as the Hollywood sign and are visible from almost anywhere in Southern California on a clear day. Many television and radio stations use the mountain for their relay signals.

Oddly enough, the marine layer that surrounds Los Angeles traps smog, making Mount Wilson a great place for a specific type of astronomy called interferometry. Of course, all the light and air pollution in the region hinder other types of astronomy.

The construction of the observatory and its telescopes brought curiosity. Along with interest came people. The Mount Wilson Toll Road was built on the mountain in 1891. It led visitors up to the mountain from Altadena for a fee. Although vehicular traffic was possible, the road was difficult to navigate, and most visitors traveled via horseback or on foot. The road is still open to traffic of a more pedestrian nature, including horses and bicyclists. This hike explores part of the old road and the landmarks that once marked the region as a major tourist attraction.

The hike is a simple trek from one mountain to the summit of another small summit on the same ridge. From the small parking area at the end of the Mount Wilson one-way loop, turn right onto the gated old Mount Wilson Toll Road. Follow the road as it descends past the remnants of an old resort camp. Some stone walls and foundations are the only things that remain. Continue to the small saddle between the two peaks.

At 1.0 mile continue straight and right toward the summit of Mount Harvard. The old toll road continues down toward Altadena on the left. Ascend to the summit and enjoy the views of Southern California on a clear day. Return via the same route.

Miles and Directions

0.0 Head down the gated entrance to the Mount Wilson Toll Road.

1.0 Reach the junction with the road up to Mount Harvard, turn right, and continue toward the summit.

1.5 Reach the summit of Mount Harvard. Return via the same route.

3.0 Arrive back at the parking area.

Pasadena and San Gabriel Foothills

Pasadena is famous not only for the little old lady in the Beach Boys song, but also the Tournament of Roses, the Rose Bowl, California Institute of Technology, and the Jet Propulsion Laboratory among others. Unbeknownst to many, however, is that the city is also a great destination for outdoor activities. Nestled at the base of the Angeles National Forest, Pasadena is the San Gabriel Valley's cultural and economic center. The name itself means "of the valley," though the designation does not come from the local Tongva tongue, but rather a non-native Midwestern language voted on by the city's founders.

Pasadena is both old and new. The feel of the city is very much modern but also refined and somehow more Spanish in scope than other cities in Los Angeles County. The hilly neighborhoods have a rugged feel, with roads headed north giving way to steep mountains and trails. In fact, the front side of the San Gabriels caused even John Muir to muse, "In the mountains of San Gabriel, overlooking the lowland vines and fruit groves, Mother Nature is most ruggedly, thornily savage. Not even in the Sierra have I ever made the acquaintance of mountains more rigidly inaccessible."

The foothills, especially where the hikes in this book are located, are a mixture of open mountain slopes covered in coastal chaparral, wide expansive views, and wild riparian canyons. The arroyos mentioned here are filled with flowing creeks and lovely waterfalls. Beautiful treasures await those intrepid souls ready to explore. None of the savagery of Muir's day exists, as trails have been built and thoroughly maintained, though the rugged access to wilderness is just a short jaunt away.

The trails located in this section can all be found within close proximity to the city of Pasadena. They demonstrate and exemplify the beauty of the surrounding region.

8 Gabrielino Trail

Enjoy an historic trail that snakes its way up the Arroyo Seco, traversing through one of Southern California's most beautiful riparian canyons.

Distance: 5.5 miles out and back

Approximate hiking time: 3 hours

Elevation gain: 600 feet

Trail surface: Packed dirt and some pavement

Best season: Spring; summer can be very hot

Other trail users: Joggers, dogs, horses, strollers, bicyclists

Canine compatibility: Dogs permitted on leash

Fees and permits: Adventure Pass required

Maps: *USGS Pasadena, CA Topo, CD 10*

Contact: Angeles National Forest, 701 N. Santa Anita Ave., Arcadia, CA 91006; (626) 574-5200; www.fs.fed.us/r5/angeles/

Finding the trailhead: From the junction of Interstate 210 and Highway 134, drive west on I-210 for 2.7 miles and take the Arroyo Boulevard exit toward Windsor Avenue. Turn right onto North Arroyo Boulevard/Windsor Avenue, drive 0.8 mile, and park in the large lot on the left. GPS: N 34 11.39' / W 118 10.01'

The Hike

This excellent hike features a vast rugged canyon, rolling streams, mini-waterfalls, and dense forest and begins near two of the city's most significant sites: the Devils Gate Reservoir and Jet Propulsion Laboratory.

Arroyo Seco is one of the Angeles National Forest's most historic and heavily visited regions. During the "golden age"

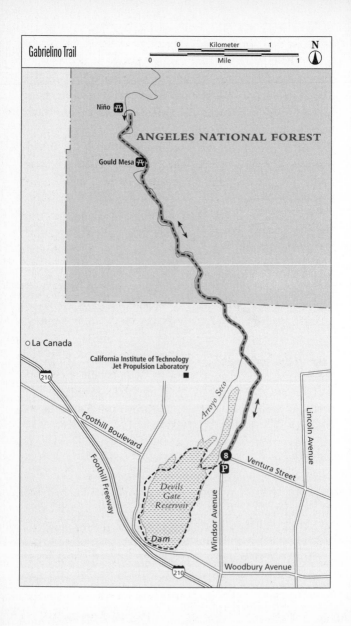

of hiking from the late 1800s through the 1930s, hikers routinely trekked from Pasadena through Arroyo Seco Canyon to the upper reaches of the San Gabriel Mountains. The hike was long, dusty, and wild. Resorts and campsites lined the way to Switzer's Camp. The area was a getaway from the hustle and hurly-burly of Los Angeles city life. Most of the remnants of the old camps and resorts have long since vanished, though the trail itself still works its way up the old road, and some foundations can be found and explored by those searching for a bit of California's past.

Today the area still teems and bustles with activity, and with good reason. The canyon is a lovely sylvan glen bursting with oak, maple, alder, bay, and sycamore trees. Nearer to the city the arroyo is definitively dry in many spots unless you're visiting during the rainy season. As the canyon ascends up into the steep foothills, water becomes more plentiful, filling in lovely brooks and cascading throughout the year.

Summers are hot and smoggy so the best time to visit is spring, when wildflowers teem in the wash. Wallflower, yarrow, yerba santa, nightshade, monkey flower, phlox, lupine, and a swarm of other specimens illuminate the region in a host of colors, making it a great place for photography, budding botanists, and children.

The route is easy to follow. From the parking area, head up Windsor for 0.25 mile and follow the thin, gated road on the right. Stay to the right as the road forks again in 0.5 mile. The road is paved for the first mile until it passes some forest service buildings and changes to a dirt road through the canyon. Here, take the left fork and follow the trail marked by a sign for the Gabrielino Trail into the creek bed.

The trail is designated as a National Recreation Trail for the benefit and enjoyment of everyone. Such trails are jointly administered by the forest service and the National Park Service under the National Trails System Act of 1968. The act was a great conservation effort designed to protect the natural history and heritage of the United States. Follow the trail as it snakes its way past campgrounds to Nino Picnic Area, the turnaround spot for this hike.

Those with more energy can continue further up the creek bed all the way into the mountains, but most people will be satisfied with this easy and pleasing adventure.

Miles and Directions

0.0 Walk north on Windsor Road.

0.25 Take the narrow road on the right, the road to the left leads to the JPL parking lot.

0.5 At the fork continue on the road to the right.

1.0 Pass some forest service buildings and continue left onto the dirt road into the canyon.

2.5 Reach Gould Mesa Campground.

2.75 Reach Niño Picnic Area. Return via the same route.

5.5 Arrive back at the parking area.

⑨ Hahamongna Watershed Park

Visit Los Angeles County's first, historic flood-control dam and the remarkable valley that surrounds it, and enjoy its beautiful riparian habitat.

Distance: 2.25-mile loop
Approximate hiking time: 1.5 hours
Elevation gain: 50 feet
Trail surface: Packed dirt and asphalt
Best season: Fall through spring
Other trail users: Bicycles, dogs, joggers, horses, strollers, wheelchairs, Frisbee enthusiasts
Canine compatibility: Leashed

dogs permitted
Fees and permits: None
Maps: *USGS Pasadena, CA Topo,* CD 9
Contact: City of Pasadena Human Services and Recreation, 100 N. Garfield Ave., Pasadena, CA 91109; (626) 744-7275; www.ci.pasadena.ca.us/human services/parksandfacilities .asp#10

Finding the trailhead: From the junction of Interstate 210 and Highway 134, drive west on I-210 for 2.7 miles and take the Arroyo Boulevard exit toward Windsor Avenue. Turn right onto North Arroyo Boulevard/Windsor Avenue, drive 0.8 mile, and park in the large lot on the left. More parking is available off Oak Grove Drive and Foothill Boulevard. GPS: N 34 11.35' / W 118 10.05'

The Hike

Hahamongna Watershed is an incredible piece of land nestled between Altadena and La Cañada Flintridge. Once known as Oak Grove Park, the area is a mecca for recreation of all sorts. Baseball diamonds, a golf course, even an eighteen-hole Frisbee golf course grace the park and its environs.

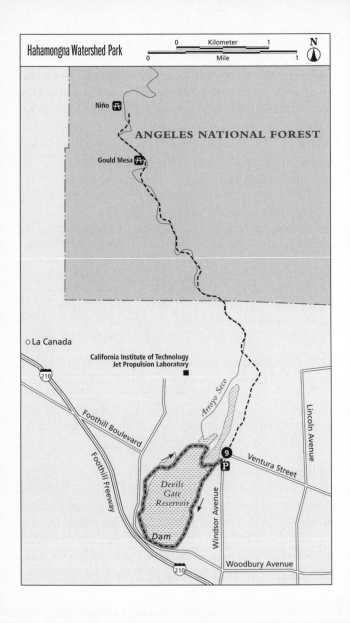

Hahamongna Watershed Park

0   Kilometer   1

0   Mile   1

N

Niño

ANGELES NATIONAL FOREST

Gould Mesa

o La Canada

California Institute of Technology
Jet Propulsion Laboratory

210

Foothill Boulevard

Foothill Freeway

Arroyo Seco

Lincoln Avenue

9
P

Ventura Street

Devils
Gate
Reservoir

Windsor Avenue

Dam

210

Woodbury Avenue

The hike skirts the edge of the Devils Gate Dam and Reservoir, which provides a habitat for wildlife, including birds. Specifically, the region is noted as the habitat of the endangered southwestern arroyo toad, and a massive plan to implement development in the Hahamongna Watershed had to be altered and postponed due to the creature's presence here. The park is a wonderful place to visit, and those interested in the history of Southern California should be particularly intrigued.

The Devils Gate was the first flood-control dam in Los Angeles County built to stop severe flooding in the Arroyo Seco wash and its confluence with the Los Angeles River. Major flooding in 1914 and 1916 destroyed homes, bridges, and lives. The project was completed in 1920 next to a startling rock formation, which has an uncanny resemblance to a two-horned devil with a goatee. Naturally, the area is steeped in lore and mythology of a fiendish nature. Reputedly in the 1950s three separate incidents occurred in which four people were lost in the vicinity and they were never seen or heard from again. In one instance, a jacket and bicycle were found, but in others there was never any trace. Howling apparitions and other strangeness are said to have been noticed in the area, and the place was rumored to be an entrance into the very depths of hell.

From the middle of the parking area, walk north 0.1 mile on the dirt path and turn left onto the dirt trail or asphalt roadway that eventually connects with the East Rim Trail. In 0.75 mile the trail connects with the Devils Gate Dam, which can be traversed to get to the other side. Be sure to look for the ghoulish rock formation and walk across the dam. At 1.1 miles take the right fork and stay close to the reservoir area, walking along the western edge of the spillway. Here the trail leads through lovely oak woodlands. At 1.75 miles turn right and head back toward the parking area, making another right-hand turn at 1.85 miles. Take the next left and head north back to the original trail. Walking north will eventually skirt the parking area and lead back to the beginning of the loop.

Bird-watchers should be especially interested in the region as many species have been cataloged here. Wildlife is ample for an urban park, and the wildflower blossoms in the spring are wondrous.

Miles and Directions

0.0 Head north on the small trail leaving the parking area.

0.1 Turn left and head south on the trail or roadway that follows the eastern edge of the watershed.

0.75 Cross the Devils Gate Dam.

1.1 Take the right fork and skirt the edge of the wetlands.

1.75 Turn right and walk east across the spillway.

1.85 Turn right again.

2.1 Turn left and head north.

2.15 Turn right.

2.25 Arrive back at the parking area.

10 Dawn Mine

Explore wild and beautifully shaded Millard Canyon and an historic mine, plus take in views of a lovely 40-foot waterfall.

Distance: 5.2 miles out and back
Approximate hiking time: 3 hours
Elevation gain: 1,600 feet
Trail surface: Packed dirt and dirt road
Best season: Fall through spring
Other trail users: Dogs, bicycles
Canine compatibility: Leashed dogs permitted

Fees and permits: Adventure Pass required
Maps: *USGS Pasadena, CA Topo, CD 10*
Contact: Angeles National Forest, 701 N. Santa Anita Ave., Arcadia, CA 91006; (626) 574-5200; www.fs.fed.us/r5/angeles/

Finding the trailhead: From the junction of Interstate 210 and Highway 134, take I-210 west for 2.0 miles, exit at Lincoln Avenue, and turn right onto Lincoln Avenue (signed for Altadena). Drive 1.9 miles. Turn right onto West Loma Alta Drive and follow it for 0.6 mile. Turn left onto Chaney Trail, drive for 1.1 miles, and park along the roadway. GPS: N 34 12.55' / W 118 08.49'

The Hike

The hike to Dawn Mine through Millard Canyon is one of the most underutilized and understated stretches of the Angeles National Forest—natural beauty absolutely flourishes here. The atmosphere is truly stunning. Not only is the gorgeous riparian splendor copious, history abounds in the area as well. Visitors can look forward to seeing remnants of the mine and its operation throughout the canyon, along

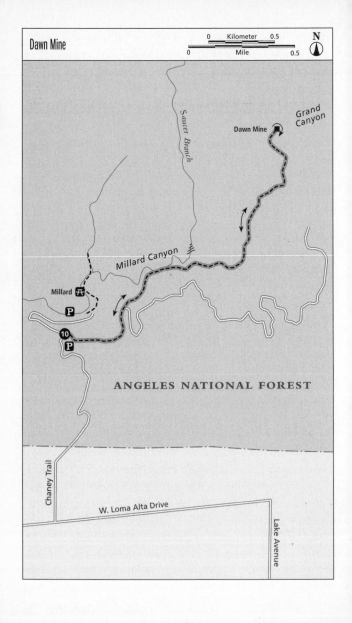

Dawn Mine

Saucer Branch

Dawn Mine

Grand Canyon

Millard Canyon

Millard

P

10
P

ANGELES NATIONAL FOREST

Chaney Trail

W. Loma Alta Drive

Lake Avenue

with the beautiful cascade of Saucer Falls. Hikers can expect to see some other people, but the area isn't extremely popular, especially once the trail branches up-canyon.

The mine itself was worked on and off for more than fifty years, spanning from the 1890s to the 1950s. Small scores were made, but no big strikes were in store for the mostly luckless prospectors in the region. The mine was closed in the mid-1950s and boarded up, but no such barriers remain today. It should be noted that spelunking is dangerous, and the water-filled tunnels contain many hazards both seen and unseen.

From Chaney Trail, head right at the locked gate onto Sunset Ridge Fire Road. Follow the road for 300 feet and meet a junction marked for Altadena Crest Trail. The trail that heads north leads to the Millard Canyon Campground: Ignore it and continue down the road for 0.15 mile. Here a signed trail marked Sunset Ridge Trail leaves the road to the north. Take the trail and follow it as it snakes into Millard Canyon. After a short distance the sound of Millard Canyon Falls can be heard when water is flowing through the canyon. The trail arcs around and reaches a curve with a viewpoint of Saucer Falls, which cascades 40 to 50 feet over the edge of a cliff. There are actually several drops but not all are visible. The trail descends gently into the canyon and after a mile of hiking comes to a junction. Take the left path at the signed Sunset Trail. This trail immediately takes the hiker over a metal bridge that appears to be crafted from discarded mine junk and leads past a cabin on the right. From there, the trail drops and enters into Millard Canyon.

The trail remains in good shape for a stretch, but it eventually becomes washed out and only fragments of trail remain. Hikers will have to trek through the canyons, crossing the creek, rock hopping, and watching for the trail as well as abundant poison oak. There are too many crossings to count and eventually even those determined to keep track will lose count. A small use trail enters from the left at the base of Saucer Canyon. Stay to the right and continue in the main canyon as it wraps north. Climb the eastern hillside and avoid the boulder-choked gorge. After climbing over and around this obstacle, the trail leads up toward the mine.

Avoid side trails and notice the rusted mining remains that become more and more pronounced. Continue forward under the water pipe, and the mine is just a little ways ahead. Two steel girders jut out of the rock and mark the entrance to the mine. Walk past the beams and continue around the rock to the hole in the earth known as Dawn Mine. Entering the mine is not recommended. Return via the same route.

Miles and Directions

0.0 Park along the roadway, but do not block the gate. Head east along Sunset Ridge Fire Road.

0.25 Turn left onto the trail marked Sunset Ridge.

1.0 Arrive at a junction, head left, and cross the bridge over a drainage. A cabin will be just ahead on the right. Follow the canyon and the loosely defined trail.

2.6 Arrive at the mine entrance. Retrace your steps to finish the hike.

5.2 Arrive back at the parking area.

11 Millard Canyon Falls

Enjoy a short and easy walk through a canyon to a lovely grotto and easily accessible waterfall.

Distance: 1.5 miles out and back
Approximate hiking time: 1 hour
Elevation gain: 150 feet
Trail surface: Packed dirt, rock
Best season: Late fall through early spring; hot in summer
Other trail users: Joggers, dogs
Canine compatibility: Leashed dogs permitted

Fees and permits: Adventure Pass required
Maps: USGS Pasadena, CA Topo, CD 10
Contact: Angeles National Forest, 701 N. Santa Anita Ave., Arcadia, CA 91006; (626) 574-5200; www.fs.fed.us/r5/angeles/

Finding the trailhead: From the junction of Interstate 210 and Highway 134, take I-210 west for 2.0 miles, exit at Lincoln Avenue, and turn right onto Lincoln Avenue (signed for Altadena). Drive 1.9 miles. Turn right onto West Loma Alta Drive and follow it for 0.6 mile. Turn left onto Chaney Trail and drive 1.1 miles to the junction with Sunset Ridge Road. Turn left and drive 0.5 mile to the campground and day-use parking. The trail begins at the rear of the parking area. GPS: N 34 12.59' / W 118 08.42'

The Hike

Follow the road through the parking lot east and north toward the creek. There is a sign with an arrow that clearly marks the route. The trail is easy to follow and great for people of all ages; its short distance and grand finish will give neophytes or those simply looking to stretch their legs a purpose and a finite conclusion for just a little bit of work.

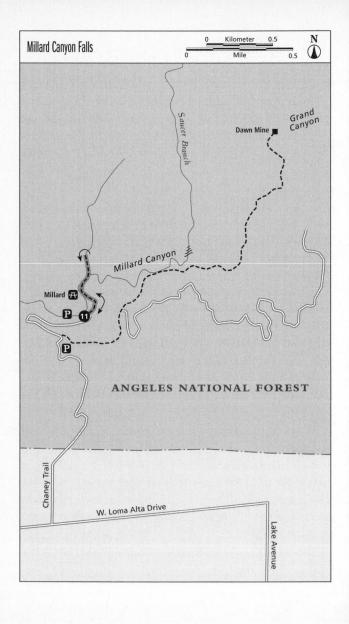

Millard Canyon Falls

N

0   Kilometer   0.5

0   Mile   0.5

Saucer Branch

Grand Canyon

Dawn Mine

Millard Canyon

Millard

P

11

P

ANGELES NATIONAL FOREST

Chaney Trail

W. Loma Alta Drive

Lake Avenue

This trip is somewhat popular, especially on weekends when the falls are flowing. Water tumbles through the shaded canyon, creating a placid and charming effect that seems to place Millard Canyon far away from the suburban sprawl of the San Gabriel Valley. In reality the canyon and its falls are very close to civilization, which is one of the reasons this place is so popular. However, it isn't likely to be overcrowded, and visitors will almost always offer a friendly hello to passersby. Those sharing in the charm and beauty of the canyon almost seem to regale in the fact that this little slice of beauty is a secret kept by those who travel here, and the place feels more protected because of this. There seems to be less trash and graffiti here than in other, more accessible and well-known areas.

Walk up the path from the parking lot and cross a small rock dam. The trail is easy to follow, though there are some very minor rock crossings that have to be made to get to the falls. Wandering along the creek, visitors will enjoy shade from oak, laurel, maple, and alder. A short half mile from the entrance, visitors come to the edge of the falls, though their distinctive tumble can be heard a bit sooner. The flow of water above the falls has been diverted for use as drinking water, so there is never a cataract present. The creek flows best after spring rains. Fall, when the leaves change color, is also a beautiful time to visit, but water is often absent before the onset of rains. Even in the best of times, the falls merely trickle over the edge, but a nice pool is present nearly year-round. Enjoy the serenity and return the same way you came.

Miles and Directions

0.0 Park in the parking lot. Walk east and north through the campground.

0.25 Start up the trail at the signed entrance.

0.75 Arrive at the waterfall and hike's terminus. Return via the same route.

1.5 Arrive back at the parking area.

12 Echo Mountain

Wander through the foothills above Altadena to historic Echo Mountain. Take in clear sky views and visit markers and relics from earlier times.

Distance: 5.0 miles out and back

Approximate hiking time: 2.5 hours

Elevation gain: 1,500 feet

Trail surface: Packed dirt

Best season: Late fall through early spring; hot in summer

Other trail users: Dogs, bicycles, joggers

Canine compatibility: Leashed dogs allowed

Fees and permits: None

Maps: USGS Mount Wilson, CA Topo, CD 9

Contact: Angeles National Forest, 701 N. Santa Anita Ave., Arcadia, CA 91006; (626) 574-5200; www.fs.fed.us/r5/angeles/

Finding the trailhead: From the junction of Interstate 210 and Highway 134, take I-210 east for 0.6 mile and exit at Lake Avenue. Turn left onto Lake Avenue and follow it north for 3.7 miles to its end at Loma Alta Drive. Park along the roadway. GPS: N 34 12.15' / W 118 07.46'

The Hike

The summit of Echo Mountain lords over the Altadena skyline. Once home to the historic Mount Lowe Railway and the White City Resort, the trek to the top of Echo Mountain is now solely a pedestrian venture best suited for the cool days of winter when skies are azure and the temperature is cool. Mostly sun exposed, the route is best to be avoided during the heat of the day, and hiking during summertime other than near dawn or dusk is folly due to temperatures and smog. Echo Mountain was named because

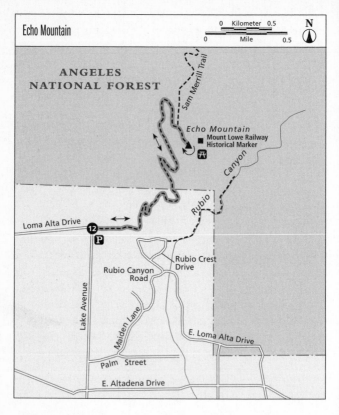

of its incredible sonic capabilities; the canyons that surround the peak are excellent for carrying waves of sound.

On clear days the hike presents a stunning panorama of the Los Angeles Basin and the shiny blue Pacific. The trip follows the lower portion of the Sam Merrill Trail as it snakes its way to the wide summit, lined with historical markers and plaques. The so-called White City that stood atop the peak was actually made up of several buildings and an observatory all painted white, which were clearly visible from the city below. Two hotels stood atop the peak, one a seventy-room mansion, the other a forty-room chalet. Today some scattered foundations, stairs, leftover mechanical relics, and various bits of rubble are the only remnants of a bygone era in the Angeles National Forest.

From the late 1890s through the 1930s, funicular rail cars shuttled passengers from Altadena up to the crest of the San Gabriel Mountains. Indeed, the railway was a prime tourist attraction in Southern California. Fires, floods, difficult access, and prohibitive prices all led to the railway's decline and eventual abandonment, but numerous organizations have contributed to keeping its legacy and history intact. The trail is remarkably well maintained and frequently used.

From the terminus of Lake Avenue, walk east along the fenced road past the stone gateway. Continue straight along the fence as the paved road curves to the north to the sign for the Sam Merrill Trail. The trail enters Los Flores Canyon heading north, switchbacking and winding up the steep slope of Echo Mountain. The trail is easy to follow and the summit is impossible to miss. Continue up toward the top and be on the lookout for remnants of the old railway and resorts. Atop the summit enjoy the placards and history, and then return via the same route.

Miles and Directions

0.0   From Lake Avenue, walk east beyond the stone gateway along a chain-link fence.

0.1   Stay straight and enter the Sam Merrill Trail. Continue toward the top.

2.5   Arrive at the summit of Echo Mountain. Return via the same route.

5.0   Arrive back at Lake Avenue parking.

13 Rubio Canyon

Hike up a rugged canyon to several lovely waterfalls.

Distance: 1.5 miles out and back

Approximate hiking time: 1 hour

Elevation gain: 500 feet

Trail surface: Packed dirt and rock

Best season: Late fall through early spring

Other trail users: Dogs

Canine compatibility: Leashed dogs allowed

Fees and permits: None

Maps: *USGS Mount Wilson, CA Topo,* CD 9

Contact: Angeles National Forest, 701 N. Santa Anita Ave., Arcadia, CA 91006; (626) 574-5200; www.fs.fed.us/r5/angeles/

Finding the trailhead: From the junction of Interstate 210 and Highway 134, head east on I-210 for 0.5 mile. Exit at Lake Avenue and turn left. Head north for 2.9 miles. Turn right onto East Palm Street and drive for 0.2 mile. Continue straight as Palm becomes Maiden Lane for 0.3 mile. Make a slight right onto Rubio Canyon Road. Drive for 0.1 mile and veer left to stay on Rubio Canyon Road. Continue for 0.2 mile. Turn left onto Rubio Crest Drive. Drive for 0.3 mile. At the sharp right, Rubio Crest Drive becomes Pleasantridge Drive. Continue for 0.2 mile to the corner. Park on the street. The trailhead is between two houses. GPS: N 34 12.10' / N 118 07.19'

The Hike

Rubio Canyon meanders up from Altadena around the backside of Echo Mountain. The canyon was once the site of nine glorious waterfalls that could be reached via a series of stairwells. In the late 1800s the Mount Lowe Railway wound through the canyon up to the crest of the San Gabriel Mountains, passing by the glory of the cascading water.

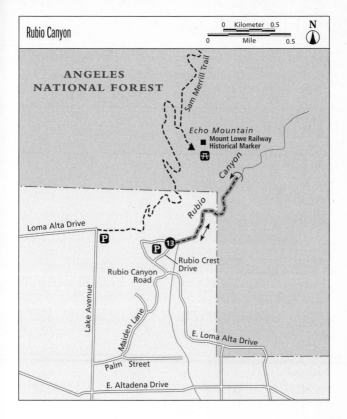

Rubio Canyon

In 1998 one of the most horrendous and neglectful occurrences in the history of the Angeles National Forest occurred, which wiped out several of the falls in a shower of detritus. The Rubio Canyon Land and Water Association, in an attempt to fix or replace a water pipeline, began dynamiting and back-hoeing the upper walls of the canyon. This activity knocked an avalanche into the gorge and completely covered five of the magnificent falls, marring the appearance of the canyon forever. It appeared that this egregious act of ignorance and hubris would never be repaired or redressed. To this day, the company has not been held responsible for its transgression despite lawsuits and outrage by both environmental organizations and homeowners.

However, Mother Nature acted up in October of 2004. An incredible deluge of rain battered the canyon. Some 10 inches fell in the chasm within a few hours. The resulting water forced the debris further down-canyon and uncovered the waterfalls buried in the previous debacle. Unfortunately, three of the lower falls—Maidenhair, Cavity Chute, and Bay Arbor Falls—were subsequently covered by the down-rushing debris that was flushed out of the upper canyon.

Follow the trail between the houses and along Rubio Canyon above the creek and wash. In a little over 0.5 mile, the trail descends down to the stream bed to where the three lower falls once dumped water in beautiful succession. From here, the trail becomes a bit obscured and hikers must scuttle over rocks up the canyon for another quarter of a mile to reach the base of the two-tiered splendor of Ribbon Rock and Moss Grotto Falls. This is the turnaround point for the hike. Return via the same route.

Several other falls are close by and hikers with more energy can choose to continue up canyon, but be advised that loose rocks and slippery slopes abound.

Miles and Directions

0.0 Park on Pleasantridge Drive. Walk between the two houses on the signed trail.

0.5 Descend to the creek bed and follow the canyon upwards.

0.75 Arrive at the base of Ribbon Rock Falls. Return via the same route.

1.5 Arrive back on Pleasantridge Drive.

14 Arboretum

Visit Lake Baldwin and wander through the wilds of the Los Angeles County Arboretum, enjoying wildlife and native and exotic plants.

Distance: 3-mile loop
Approximate hiking time: 3 hours at a leisurely pace
Elevation gain: 100 feet
Trail surface: Packed dirt and asphalt
Best season: Year-round
Other trail users: Wheelchairs, strollers
Canine compatibility: No dogs allowed

Fees and permits: Sliding fee is charged, depending on age.
Maps: *USGS Mount Wilson, CA Topo,* CD 9
Contact: Los Angeles County Arboretum and Botanic Garden, 301 N. Baldwin Ave., Arcadia, CA 91007; (626) 821-3222; www.arboretum.org

Finding the trailhead: From the junction of Interstate 210 and Highway 134, head east on I-210 for 5.2 miles. Exit Baldwin Avenue and turn right. Drive for 0.4 mile and enter the driveway on the right for the parking lot. GPS: N 34 08.36' / W 118 03.02'

The Hike

The Los Angeles County Arboretum and Botanical Garden is a lovely 127-acre sprawling oasis set at the base of the San Gabriel Mountains. The garden serves as a center for programs, lectures, seminars, expositions, and even concerts. While not truly a hiking destination per se, the idyllic setting and gorgeous displays of plants provides a more than stunning locale for an outdoor experience.

Visitors to the arboretum can spend hours just observing the different flora, which are categorized, labeled, and

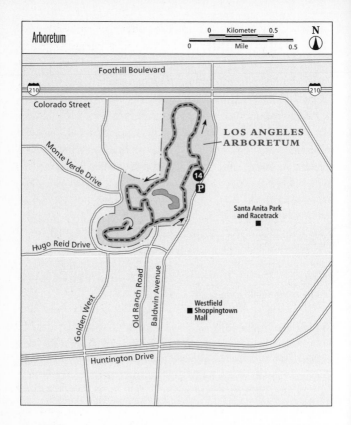

divided into sections. Groupings of plants are conveniently separated so that those walking around the grounds can experience what each different ecosystem and representative section of the earth might look like. Areas of the globe exhibited in the park are Australia, Africa, South America, the American Southwest, and Asia. Specific gardens are also designed for irises, roses, redwoods, a parcel dedicated to herbs, and a section devoted entirely to the endemic plants of the island of Madagascar. Truly a botany enthusiast's delight, the gardens have much to offer. An enjoyable visit can be had just wandering around the immense property looking at statuary, fountains, peacocks, other fauna, and the magnificent landscaping, which includes the Meyberg Waterfall.

The arboretum is a great getaway just about any day or time of year. Rarely crowded, those strolling through the premises will feel a sense of peace and solitude. In summer the heat can be stifling in certain parts of the preserve, but most regions are heavily shaded and provide for some shelter from the temperature. Certain attractions are positively stunning. Snuggled beside Lake Baldwin, the Queen Anne Cottage will most certainly conjure visions of days of old. The Victorian structure is grandiose and magnificent. It will likely seem familiar to most visitors, and that is because it is memorable from multiple movies and television series—most notably the facade served as the mansion from the popular 1970s TV series *Fantasy Island*. The lake has also been a surrogate for tropical locales in movies such as *Road to Singapore,* as well as Johnny Weissmuller's *Tarzan* series.

The hike as designated on the map is merely a suggestion and focuses on hitting all of the major highlights of the garden. In most cases it circumscribes areas that are full of smaller trails. It is encouraged for visitors to explore these areas. Sticking to a general loop path will help in getting to every major area, but take time and invent your own route.

Miles and Directions

0.0 Leave the parking area north through the admission gates. Start north and walk in a counterclockwise loop pattern through the gardens.

3.0 Arrive back at the parking area.

15 Sturtevant Falls

Hike up Big Santa Anita Canyon along a colorful stream and past old cabins to a lovely 50-foot waterfall.

Distance: 3.5 miles out and back

Approximate hiking time: 2 hours

Elevation gain: 900 feet

Trail surface: Packed dirt and asphalt

Best season: Late fall through spring

Other trail users: Dogs, horses, joggers

Canine compatibility: Leashed dogs allowed

Fees and permits: Adventure Pass required

Maps: *USGS Mount Wilson, CA Topo,* CD 9

Contact: Angeles National Forest, 701 N. Santa Anita Ave., Arcadia, CA 91006; (626) 574-5200; www.fs.fed.us/r5/angeles/

Finding the trailhead: To reach Chantry Flat from the intersection of Interstate 210 and Highway 134, drive east on I-210 for 6.4 miles. Take the Santa Anita Avenue exit and turn left onto Santa Anita Avenue. Drive north for 5.0 miles to the parking area for Chantry Flat. GPS: N 34 11.43' / W 118 01.17'

The Hike

Start hiking across the road from the lower parking area. The route is signed for the Gabrielino Trail. Chantry Flat is the eastern terminus of the 28.5-mile National Recreational Trail that winds up through Santa Anita Canyon along the San Gabriel River and back down through the Arroyo Seco. The route begins on an old paved road and descends 400 feet into the bottom of the canyon. After the short descent, the trail turns north and follows the gorge up toward the falls. Private cabins built in the early 1900s line the route nearly the entire way to the cascade. These lodges are still occupied by owners lucky enough to have their own piece of this sylvan paradise.

The route to Sturtevant Falls is rather popular, and the parking lot at the trailhead is almost always loaded with vehicles. Families, joggers, hikers, backpackers, and those out for a casual stroll head to the lovely oak-lined canyon simply to enjoy its radiant beauty. The trail is an easy getaway from the cacophony of the city. At times it is difficult to believe the roar of industrialization is so close. With all of the people, vacation homes, and various dams in the canyon, the mark of humankind is never absent, but the glen is tranquil and beautiful nonetheless.

Except during the driest years, water flows in the creek most of the time. Thus, the pacifying sound of a running stream is a constant treat. Even the flood-control dams, which were built after the horrendous deluge of 1938, do not detract from the fern-lined, wildflower-filled canyon.

From the trailhead, the thin paved road descends for half a mile into Santa Anita Canyon. Turn right at the junction with the Winter Creek Trail, and cross a bridge. The route becomes dirt and abruptly turns north and follows the creek. In a short distance the road becomes a proper trail. At 1.25 miles in, the route reaches Fiddler's Crossing. Turn right and follow the trail to the base of the falls. The trail crosses the creek a few times, though traversing the water is never very difficult except during times of high runoff.

The trail is perfectly signed—at every junction there is no confusion as to which direction to follow. It is simple to just follow the signs to get to the falls and back again.

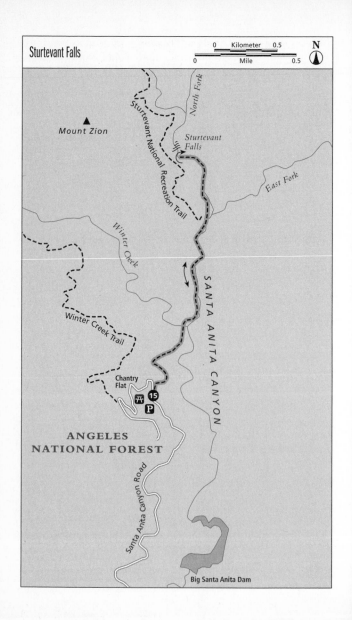

Enjoy the splendor of the 50-foot cascade along with all of the other adventurers who are likely to be taking in the sights as well.

Miles and Directions

0.0 From the lower parking area, cross the road and head down the paved section of the Gabrielino Trail.

0.5 Turn right at the junction with the Winter Creek Trail and follow Santa Anita Canyon North.

1.25 Turn right at Fiddler's Crossing and head to the base of Sturtevant Falls.

1.75 Arrive at the base of the falls. Return via the same route.

3.5 Arrive back at Chantry Flat.

16 Monrovia Canyon

Walk through lovely Monrovia Canyon Park to a glorious waterfall on this easy hike that's suitable for the entire family.

Distance: 1.5 miles out and back
Approximate hiking time: 1 hour
Elevation gain: 600 feet
Trail surface: Packed dirt
Best season: Late fall through spring
Other trail users: Dogs
Canine compatibility: Leashed dogs permitted

Fees and permits: Parking fee per vehicle; closed Tuesday
Maps: USGS Azuza, CA Topo, CD 9
Contact: Monrovia Canyon Park, 1200 N. Canyon Blvd., Monrovia, CA 91016; (626) 256-8282; www.monroviacanyonpark.org

Finding the trailhead: From the intersection of Interstate 210 and Highway 134, head east on I-210 and drive for 6.7 miles. Exit at Santa Anita Avenue and turn left. Drive for 0.2 mile and turn right onto Foothill Boulevard. Drive for 2.0 miles and turn left onto Canyon Boulevard. Drive for 1.8 miles to the entrance for Monrovia Canyon Park. Follow the road to its end and park in front of the nature center. GPS: N 34 10.32' / W 117 59.22'

The Hike

Monrovia Canyon Park is a shining forested gem. Several trails grace the park, but without a doubt the one that packs the biggest punch is the hike from the nature center to Monrovia Canyon Falls. It is also the easiest hike in the park. The trail is simple to follow, great for children, mostly free of human ugliness, and relatively untrodden for a hike so close to the confines of civilization. People say hello as

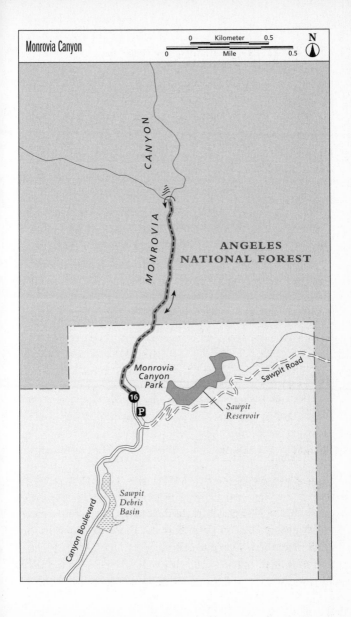

Monrovia Canyon

0   Kilometer   0.5
0   Mile   0.5

N

CANYON

MONROVIA

ANGELES
NATIONAL FOREST

Monrovia
Canyon
Park

16

P

Sawpit Road

Sawpit
Reservoir

Sawpit
Debris
Basin

Canyon Boulevard

they pass by, which is unusual for an urban park with such a large amount of pedestrian traffic. There are also four picnic areas located within the park.

Thankfully there is very little graffiti, though a few trees have been unkindly scarred by those who do not know any better. A few stone steps have been carved out of the rock along the narrow and steady uphill trail, but they seem fairly natural as far as improvements go. There are also a few embankments beside the creek used to control the flow of water in order to ease erosion along the trail. The route follows the riparian canyon through dense oak, alder, maple, sycamore, and scattered pine, climbing ever upward toward the 50-foot cascade at the trail's conclusion. The route is steady yet never steep, always shaded, and comfortably cool even in the heat of summer. A family of deer sometimes wander along the trail, and the beauty of the park is simply exquisite. This is one of those places that feels more remote than it actually is. Enjoy the tranquillity of the falls, then return via the same route.

Those interested would do well to visit the nature center before a hike. The friendly staff are available to answer questions about the region's history and the local flora and fauna. Displays on-site will also help people in identifying common vegetation. Be sure to leave the park before the gate closes at 5:00 p.m.

Miles and Directions

0.0 Begin hiking behind the nature center.

1.25 Arrive at Monrovia Canyon Falls. Return via the same route.

1.5 Arrive back at the nature center.

17 Fish Canyon

Hike to one of the San Gabriel's loveliest waterfalls. The 80-foot, three-tiered cascade puts on a tremendous display.

Distance: 3.0 miles out and back
Approximate hiking time: 1.5 hours
Elevation gain: 500 feet
Trail surface: Packed dirt
Best season: Late fall through early spring
Other trail users: Dogs
Canine compatibility: Leashed dogs allowed
Fees and permits: Access to the trailhead is controlled by Vulcan Materials Company. Hikers must make arrangements for a shuttle to hike to the falls.
Maps: USGS Azusa, CA Topo, CD 9
Contact: Vulcan Materials Company, 1200 Urban Center Dr., Birmingham, AL 35242; (626) 633-4238 or (323) 474-3208; www.azusarock.com

Finding the trailhead: From the intersection of Interstate 210 and Highway 134, take I-210 east for 11.2 miles. Exit at Mount Olive Drive/Interstate 605, merge onto I-605 north, and drive for 0.6 mile. Turn right onto Huntington Drive. Drive for 0.6 mile. Turn left onto Encanto Parkway. Drive for 1.6 miles to the parking area on the left. Take the shuttle to the trailhead. GPS: N 34 09.53' / W 117 55.29'

The Hike

Fish Canyon and its namesake waterfall were once the pride of the foothills of the San Gabriel Mountains. The falls are perhaps the most impressive of any in Southern California. Three separate drops pour water over a series of mossy cliffs into stunning pools. Hikers pre-1950s were able to park their cars and take a leisurely stroll up-canyon to the most

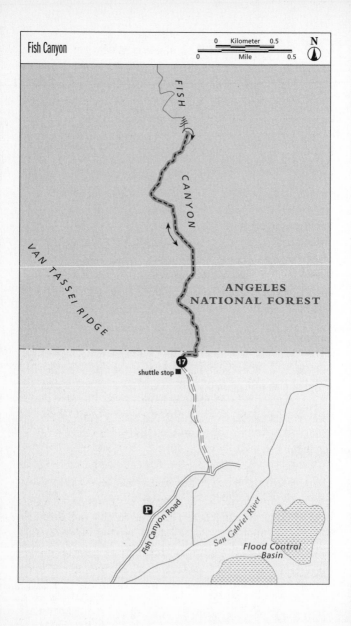

Fish Canyon

FISH

CANYON

VAN TASSEI RIDGE

ANGELES
NATIONAL FOREST

17

shuttle stop ■

Fish Canyon Road

San Gabriel River

Flood Control
Basin

0   Kilometer   0.5
0   Mile   0.5

N

sublime of spectacles. Today, the trail to the falls is much the same, but access has been severely limited by Vulcan Materials Corporation and their subsidiary Azusa Rock. The company owns the land that abuts the trailhead and the only way to reach it is through private property.

Over the past decade the corporation has done much to appease the public by offering biweekly shuttles through restricted areas to the trailhead from late fall through mid-summer. A bypass trail that avoids company property was constructed in 1998, but the route is incredibly long, difficult, and by many reports poorly planned and executed. Almost no one uses the route because of the 3,000-foot elevation gain, lack of maintenance, and the sheer steepness of the trail. Hikers, environmentalists, and outdoors enthusiasts of all sorts have clamored for more access, but it seems reasonable to believe that the situation will remain as is for as long as mining continues in the area. Do not attempt to trespass as the corporation vigorously pursues and prosecutes violators. Instead, contact the company for shuttle dates and follow set guidelines.

The hike itself starts by crossing a metal footbridge and then skirting along the trail as it leads north and upstream. Some interpretive signs are placed alongside the trail, instructing visitors about the history of the region. The trail is shadeless in spots, but as the canyon narrows, the riparian splendor of oak, spruce, alder, and sycamore provide places for respite under the arbors. Beware of poison oak, which is ubiquitous on the trail. The trail climbs and descends intermittently before it eventually drops into the creek bed just before the falls. One creek crossing is necessary, and it is possible that hikers will get wet, but most people will want to get wet anyway. Return via the same route and arrive back to the shuttle access point by 3:00 p.m., as this is when the last shuttle begins its return route.

Miles and Directions

0.0   Start north at the trailhead toward Fish Canyon Falls. Walk across the bridge and follow the creek.

1.5   Arrive at Fish Canyon Falls. Return via the same route.

3.0   Arrive back at the trailhead and the shuttle.

18 Glendora Wilderness Park

Take a hike to a high promontory with incredible views on a clear day.

Distance: 4.5 miles out and back

Approximate hiking time: 2.5 hours

Elevation gain: 1,400 feet

Trail surface: Packed dirt

Best season: Late fall through early spring

Other trail users: Dogs, cyclists, joggers

Canine compatibility: Leashed dogs permitted

Fees and permits: None

Maps: *USGS Glendora, CA Topo, CD 9*

Contact: City of Glendora, 116 E. Foothill Blvd., Glendora, CA 91741-3380; (626) 914-8200; www.ci.glendora.ca.us/ community_services/parks

---

Finding the trailhead: From the intersection of Interstate 210 and Highway 134, take I-210 east for 16.2 miles and exit north onto Grand Avenue. Drive toward the mountains for 1.7 miles and turn right onto Foothill Boulevard. Continue for 2.0 miles and turn left onto North Valley Center Avenue. Drive for 0.7 mile and turn left onto Sierra Madre Avenue. Cross over the flood-control channel and make a right onto Glendora Mountain Road. Drive for 0.7 mile to the large turnout and parking area on the left. GPS: N 34 09.24' / W 117 50.10'

The Hike

From the enormous turnout on Glendora Mountain Road, walk southeast across the roadway to where a large firebreak starts immediately and steeply up the side of the mountain. This route is informally known as the Poop–Out Trail, and that it is. In a quarter of a mile, the swath gains over 600 feet scrambling straight up the mountainside. The vertical nature of this "trail" is sure to gas and wind all except the strongest of hikers. Nearly half of the elevation gained on the entire route is out of the way in just this short span of a few hundred horizontal feet. Phew! Some hikers may want to take a sizable break here in order to catch their breath.

Views into the city and beyond begin immediately. Just after rounding the top of a small summit, unnamed peak 1,817', the route descends briefly. Ignore the use trail on the right and stay straight at the three-way junction. Here the trail evens out a bit and becomes a more steady and gradual ascent up Lower Monroe Fire Road. The service road has long been closed to motorized traffic, making this a peaceful climb.

Follow the road for the remainder of the trip. Several cutoffs and use trails, forged by those wishing to avoid switchbacks, also make their way up to the ultimate destination for this hike. At 2.25 miles, another unnamed summit sits just off the roadway as it makes a hairpin turn. Climb up any of the small use trails and reach a peak that used to be home to radio repeater towers that have since been removed. Only sparse odds and ends remain to mark their presence. From this vantage point, hikers can see all of Los Angeles, the higher country to the north, and even the Pacific Ocean and Channel Islands on clear days. Enjoy the view and return via the same route.

Miles and Directions

0.0 From the turnout, head southeast toward the guardrail and hike up the firebreak known as Poop-Out Trail.

0.3 Reach high point 1817'.

0.5 Pass a use trail on the right and continue to the three-way junction.

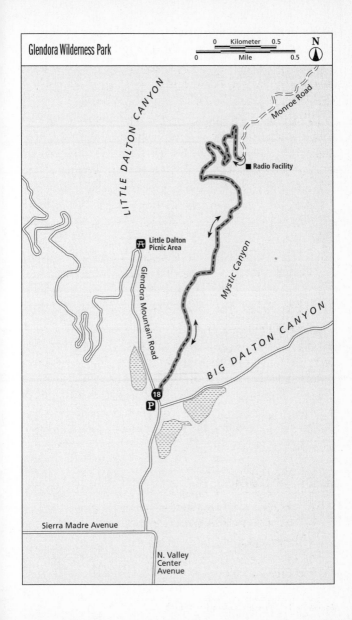

Glendora Wilderness Park

0   Kilometer   0.5

0   Mile   0.5

N

LITTLE DALTON CANYON

Monroe Road

■ Radio Facility

Mystic Canyon

Little Dalton
Picnic Area

Glendora Mountain Road

BIG DALTON CANYON

18

P

Sierra Madre Avenue

N. Valley
Center
Avenue

0.6 Continue straight and take Lower Monroe Fire Road toward another unnamed summit.

2.2 Turn right and ascend a use trail to an unnamed peak.

2.25 Arrive on top of unnamed summit. Return via the same route.

4.5 Arrive back at the parking area.

19   Claremont Hills Wilderness Park

Enjoy the open space and clear-sky views of Claremont Hills Preserve, a 1,693-acre park that sits at the base of the San Gabriel Mountains.

Distance: 4.75-mile loop
Approximate hiking time: 2.5 hours
Elevation gain: 1,100 feet
Trail surface: Packed dirt
Best season: Late fall through spring
Other trail users: Bicycles, dogs, horses, joggers

Canine compatibility: Leashed dogs permitted
Fees and permits: None
Maps: *USGS Mount Baldy, CA Topo,* CD 9
Contact: City of Claremont, 207 Harvard Ave., Claremont, CA 91711; (909) 399-5460; www .ci.claremont.ca.us/

Finding the trailhead: From the intersection of Interstate 210 and Highway 134, drive east on I-210 for 24.3 miles and exit at Towne Avenue. Turn left and drive for 0.1 mile. Turn right onto Base Line Road and drive for 1.7 miles. Turn left onto Mills Avenue and drive for 1.4 miles to its end and park in the lot on the left. GPS: N 34 08.34' / W 117 42.26'

The Hike

From the parking lot, head up Cobalt Canyon Motorway and continue straight and to the right at the first intersection with the Burbank Motorway. This road will be the return portion of your loop. The road through Cobalt Canyon climbs more gradually with greater opportunities for shade, so it is much better to ascend the loop on this side. Stately oaks line the route for the first mile, making the path up a little more idyllic than the chaparral-covered western portion of the trip. At no

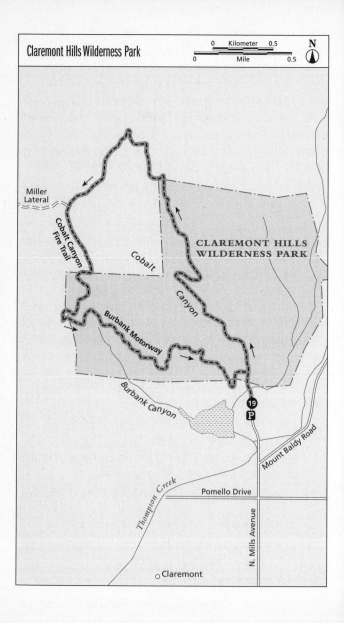

Claremont Hills Wilderness Park

0   Kilometer   0.5

0   Mile   0.5

N

Miller
Lateral

Cobalt Canyon
Fire Trail

Cobalt

Canyon

CLAREMONT HILLS
WILDERNESS PARK

Burbank Motorway

Burbank Canyon

19
P

Mount Baldy Road

Thompson Creek

Pomello Drive

N. Mills Avenue

Claremont

time is route-finding difficult as the entire trip is made on fire roads that are adequately signed.

At the next intersection, turn left onto Cobalt Canyon Fire Trail, where the road winds toward a prominent peak that can be scrambled to for an excellent 360-degree view. Stay straight at the following junction with Miller Lateral, and turn left onto the Burbank Motorway at 3.25 miles. This road returns to near the beginning of the hike. One last right turn deposits hikers and cyclists back at the parking area.

The trails in Claremont Hills Wilderness Park are favorites of mountain bikers, and there will most definitely be cyclists out on the roads. However, it is a grand place for a day hike, especially during the winter months when snow lines the upper Angeles and San Bernardino National Forests. Clear-day views stretch for miles, and when the air is crisp and cool, the park seems to be sitting on top of the world.

When winter rains have fallen, the hills become a dynamite color of green. Wildflowers blossom, igniting the foothills with vibrant oranges, blues, purples, and yellows.

Miles and Directions

0.0 Walk north up Cobalt Canyon Motorway.

0.1 Continue straight at the junction with Burbank Motorway.

1.5 Turn left onto Cobalt Canyon Fire Trail.

2.0 Reach the high point of the trail. Scramble uphill to a prominent summit and take in a 360-degree view.

2.1 Head left at the fork and continue on Cobalt Canyon Fire Trail.

2.4 Continue straight at the junction with Miller Lateral.

3.25 Turn left onto Burbank Motorway.

4.65 Turn right onto Cobalt Canyon Motorway.

4.75 Arrive back at the parking area.

About the Author

Allen Riedel is a photographer, journalist, author, and teacher. He lives with his wife, Monique, and children, Michael, Sierra, and Makaila, in Riverside, California. He writes an outdoor column for the *Press-Enterprise* and has authored several hiking guides, including *Best Hikes with Dogs: Southern California, 100 Classic Hikes in Southern California, Best Easy Day Hikes Riverside,* and *Best Easy Day Hikes San Bernardino.*